QUICK!
MISCHIEF MAKERS,
SIGN HERE so everyone
knows **this book** belongs
TO YOU.

_____

Books by Roald Dahl

THE BFG
BOY: TALES OF CHILDHOOD
BOY *and* GOING SOLO
CHARLIE AND THE CHOCOLATE FACTORY
CHARLIE AND THE GREAT GLASS ELEVATOR
THE COMPLETE ADVENTURES OF CHARLIE AND MR WILLY WONKA
DANNY THE CHAMPION OF THE WORLD
THE ENORMOUS CROCODILE
ESIO TROT
FANTASTIC MR FOX
GEORGE'S MARVELLOUS MEDICINE
THE GIRAFFE AND THE PELLY AND ME
GOING SOLO
JAMES AND THE GIANT PEACH
MATILDA
THE MAGIC FINGER
THE TWITS
THE WITCHES

Picture books
DIRTY BEASTS
THE ENORMOUS CROCODILE
THE GIRAFFE AND THE PELLY AND ME
THE MINPINS
REVOLTING RHYMES

Plays
THE BFG: PLAYS FOR CHILDREN (*Adapted by David Wood*)
CHARLIE AND THE CHOCOLATE FACTORY: A PLAY (*Adapted by Richard George*)
DANNY THE CHAMPION OF THE WORLD: PLAYS FOR CHILDREN
(*Adapted by David Wood*)
FANTASTIC MR FOX: A PLAY (*Adapted by Sally Reid*)
JAMES AND THE GIANT PEACH: A PLAY (*Adapted by Richard George*)
THE TWITS: PLAYS FOR CHILDREN (*Adapted by David Wood*)
THE WITCHES: PLAYS FOR CHILDREN (*Adapted by David Wood*)

Teenage fiction
THE GREAT AUTOMATIC GRAMMATIZATOR AND OTHER STORIES
RHYME STEW
SKIN AND OTHER STORIES
THE VICAR OF NIBBLESWICKE
THE WONDERFUL STORY OF HENRY SUGAR AND SIX MORE

Collections
THE ROALD DAHL TREASURY
SONGS AND VERSE

ROALD DAHL

WHIZZPOPPING JOKE BOOK

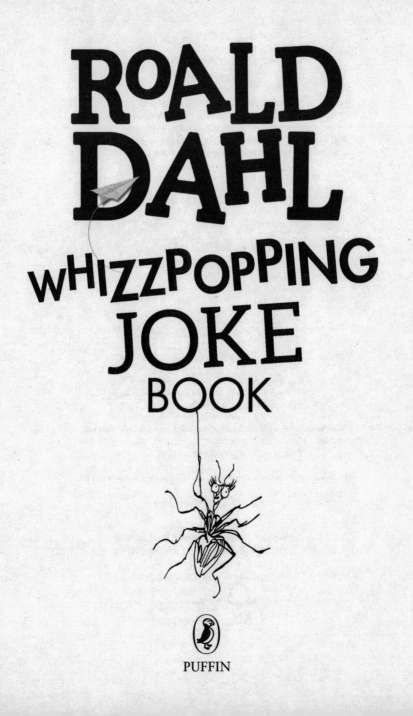

PUFFIN

PUFFIN BOOKS

UK | USA | Canada | Ireland | Australia
India | New Zealand | South Africa

Puffin Books is part of the Penguin Random House group of companies
whose addresses can be found at global.penguinrandomhouse.com.

www.penguin.co.uk
www.puffin.co.uk
www.ladybird.co.uk

Penguin
Random House
UK

First published 2016

011

Printed in Great Britain by Clays Ltd, St Ives plc

A CIP catalogue record for this book is available from the British Library

ISBN: 978–0–141–36823–8

All correspondence to:
Puffin Books, Penguin Random House Children's
80 Strand, London WC2R 0RL

ROALD DAHL was a spy, ace fighter pilot, chocolate historian and medical inventor. He was also the author of *Charlie and the Chocolate Factory*, *Matilda*, *The BFG* and many more brilliant stories. He remains **THE WORLD'S NUMBER ONE STORYTELLER.**

QUENTIN BLAKE has illustrated more than three hundred books and was Roald Dahl's favourite illustrator. In 1980 he won the prestigious Kate Greenaway Medal. In 1999 he became the first ever Children's Laureate and in 2013 he was knighted for services to illustration.

Miss Trunchbull's
BANNED school jokes

Tell these to your **friends** and you'll be thrown straight in the **chokey!**

Why did the teacher put the lights on?
Because the class was so dim!

Who invented fractions?
Henry the Eighth!

Why was Miss Trunchbull worried?
Because there were too many rulers in school!

MISS TRUNCHBULL: What do we call the outer part of a tree?
BRUCE BOGTROTTER: **Don't know, Miss!**
MISS TRUNCHBULL: Bark, silly! Bark!
BRUCE BOGTROTTER: **Woof, woof!**

Why is six afraid of seven? **Because seven eight nine!**

"If you get on the wrong side of Miss Trunchbull, she can liquidize you like a carrot in a BLENDER."

TEACHER: Make up a sentence using the word "lettuce". PUPILS: **Let us out of school early!**

TEACHER: What are you reading? PUPIL: **I dunno!** TEACHER: But you're reading aloud! PUPIL: **Yeah, but I'm not listening!**

If two's company and three's a crowd, what are four and five? **Nine!**

How did you find school today? **Well, I just got off the bus and there it was!**

TEACHER: You aren't paying attention. Are you having trouble hearing? PUPIL: **No, sir. I'm having trouble listening!**

How do bees get to school? **By school buzz!**

What is a snake's favourite subject? **Hiss-tory!**

What is an archaeologist?
Someone whose career is in ruins!

Why did the nose hate school?
It was tired of being picked on!

What happens when you take the school bus home?
The police make you bring it back!

What do elves learn in school?
The elf-abet!

What's the best way to get straight As?
Use a ruler!

What grade did the pirate get at school? **High Cs!**

Which animal cheats in school? **A cheetah!**

What's a witch's favourite subject? **Spell-ing!**

What is a pirate's favourite subject? **Arrrrrt!**

LITTLE BOY: I can't go to school today, I have a tummy ache.
MUM: **Where does it hurt?**
LITTLE BOY: In school!

How do you make the number one disappear? **Add the letter "g" and it's "gone"!**

Why did the teacher write on the window? **To make her lesson very clear!**

Why was the broom late for school? **He over-swept!**

Why didn't the skeleton go to the school dance? **He had no body to take!**

Bruce Bogtrotter's
BELLY LAUGHS

Are you ready for some **tasty** one-liners?

What's that fly doing in my gravy?
Looks like breast stroke!

What tables don't you have to learn?
Dinner tables!

What kind of nuts always seem to have a cold?
Cashews!

What is a pretzel's favourite dance?
The twist!

What are twins' favourite fruit?
Pears!

CUSTOMER: Waiter, this food tastes funny.
WAITER: **Then why aren't you laughing?**

Suddenly the boy let out a **gigantic BELCH** which rolled around the Assembly Hall like thunder. Many of the audience began to GIGGLE. "**Silence!**" shouted the Trunchbull.

What do computer operators eat for lunch?
Chips!

What would happen if pigs could fly?
The price of bacon would go up.

Waiter, will my pizza be long? **No, sir, it will be round!**

What happens if you make a walnut laugh? **It cracks up!**

Why did the banana go to the doctor? **Because it wasn't peeling well!**

What do you call a peanut in a spacesuit? **An astro-nut!**

What is green and sings? **Elvis Parsley!**

What cheese is made backwards?
Edam.

What did the nacho say to the burrito?
Can we taco 'bout it?

Why did the baker stop making doughnuts?
She was bored of the hole business!

What type of cheese doesn't belong to you?
Nacho cheese!

Knock knock!
Who's there?
Justin.
Justin who?
Justin time for lunch!

CUSTOMER: Is there spaghetti on the menu today?
WAITER: **No, I cleaned it off!**

What did the Italian chef give his waiters?
A pizza his mind!

What do polar bears have for dinner?
Iceberg-ers!

Why couldn't the teddy bear eat his lunch?
Because he was stuffed!

Why did the tomato blush?
Because it saw the salad dressing!

What did the daddy tomato say to the baby tomato?
Hurry and ketchup!

What's worse than finding a worm in your apple?
Finding half a worm in your apple!

What's orange and sounds like a parrot?
A carrot!

How do eggs leave in an emergency?
Through the fire eggs-it!

What do aliens eat off in space?
Flying saucers!

What vegetable should never be served on a boat?
Leeks!

The **Roly-Poly Bird's**
JOKEY-WOKEYS

They'll make
you **squawk!**

What is the
strongest bird?
A crane!

Why does a flamingo
lift one leg?
**Because if it
lifted both legs it
would fall over!**

Why do birds fly
south for the winter?
**Because it's too
far to walk!**

What is black,
white and red all
over?
**A sunburnt
penguin!**

What do you
call a seagull flying
over land?
A land-gull!

What do doctors give sick birds?
Tweetment!

Did you hear the joke about the broken egg?
It'll crack you up!

What's more clever than a talking bird?
A spelling bee!

What birds can you find in Portugal?
Portu-geese!

What is black and white, and black and white, and black and white, and black and white, and black and white?
A penguin rolling down a hill!

"Please don't mention Bird Pie again," said the Roly-Poly Bird. "It gives me the SHUDDERS."

Why do penguins carry fish in their beaks?
They don't have any pockets!

SON: Mum, can I have a canary for Christmas?
MUM: **No, we'll have turkey like everyone else!**

What do you call a poorly bird of prey?
Ill-eagle!

What do birds watch on TV?
Duck-umentaries!

Where do tough chickens come from?
Hard-boiled eggs!

What do you call a
bird in the winter?
Brrrrrrr-d!

What do
ducks have with
cheese?
Quackers!

What happened
when the turkey got
in a fight?
**He got the
stuffing knocked
out of him!**

Where would you find
a turkey with no legs?
**Precisely where
you left him!**

What's the most musical
part of a chicken?
The drumstick!

George's MARVELLOUS MUM JOKES

(AND **DAD** JOKES! AND **LITTLE BROTHER** JOKES! AND **GRANDMA** JOKES!)

Fun for **all** the family!

What's it called when you have your grandmother on speed dial?
Insta-gran!

What does "maximum" mean?
A very big mother!

What does "minimum" mean?
A very small mother!

DAD: Why are you sitting on the cat?
DAUGHTER: **The teacher told us to write an essay on our favourite animal!**

What did the baby corn call its father?
Pop-corn!

What did the digital watch say to the grandfather clock?
"Look, no hands!"

Why was Dad running round and round his bed?
He wanted to catch up on his sleep!

FIREMAN:
Who knows what a smoke detector is for?
LITTLE BOY:
To tell Mum when dinner is ready!

What BIG bug is related to you?
Your great aunt!

What bug is related to you?
Your aunt!

GEORGE: Mum, why is some of your hair grey?
MUM: **Every time you do something that annoys me or Dad, one of our hairs turns grey!**
GEORGE: So . . . why is *all* of Grandma's hair grey?

FRED:
My grammar's terrible!
GEORGE:
What's wrong with her?

My gran used to run an origami business, but sadly **it folded!**

Did you hear about the man who can jump from tree to tree?
He's a monkey's uncle!

Why doesn't Amy like her mum's brother?
He's a bit uncool!

GEORGE: Where are my sunglasses?
DAD: **I'm not sure. Where are my dadglasses?**

Why did the boy put a toad in his sister's bed? **Because he couldn't find a spider!**

What did Frankenstein say to his grandson when he noticed he'd got taller? **"You gruesome boy!"**

What do cannibals eat for dessert? **Chocolate-covered aunts!**

"**Mother!**" wailed Mrs Kranky. "**You've** just drunk fifty doses of GEORGE'S MARVELLOUS MEDICINE Number Four and look what one tiny spoonful did to that **little old brown hen!**" But Grandma **didn't** even hear her. Great **clouds** of steam were already **pouring** out of her mouth and she was **beginning** to **whistle**.

Why was the mummy firefly unhappy?
Her children weren't that bright!

GIRL: Dad, I want a cat for Christmas!
DAD: **You've got to be kitten me!**

PEACHY PUNS
from Around the WORLD!

These are James's **favourites** ...

What kind of biscuit would you find at the South Pole?
A penguin!

What's the difference between an American student and a UK student?
About 3,000 miles!

Did you hear about the exhausted kangaroo?
She was out of bounds!

What might you eat in Paris?
The trifle tower!

What happens when you throw a green stone in the Red Sea?
It gets wet!

What do Scotsmen eat?
Tart 'n' pie!

What is the most slippery country in the world?
Greece!

Why is Russia a very fast-moving country?
Because the people are always Russian!

What travels around the world and stays in the corner?
A stamp!

How does the sea say hello?
It waves!

How do we know that the Earth won't come to an end?
Because it's round!

Why is Dublin getting bigger?
Because it's always Dublin!

What sort of hat does a penguin wear?
An ice cap!

What pie can fly?
A magpie!

Did you hear about the wooden car with wooden wheels and a wooden engine?
It wooden go anywhere!

Which country do pirates try to sail towards?
Arrrrrrgentina!

If Ireland sank into the sea, which county would stay afloat?
Cork!

What did one flag say to the other?
Nothing, it just waved.

What did the tourist say about his trip to Cardiff?
He had a Wales of a time!

What do you call a chicken at the North Pole?
Lost!

What do people complain about when they visit Cuba?
Nothing – they're usually Havana great time!

What do you get when you cross a plane and a snake?
A Boeing constrictor!

James decided that he rather liked the CENTIPEDE. He was obviously a rascal, but what a change it was to hear somebody LAUGHING once in a while.

Where did the pencil go on holiday?
Pencil-vania!

What do you get when you cross a pilot with a wizard?
A flying sorcerer!

What should you write before going on holiday to the Czech Republic?
A Czech-list!

The Pelly's FISHY FUNNIES

These jokes **stink!**

Why do fish live in salt water?
Because pepper makes them sneeze!

Where do killer whales go to hear music?
The orca-stra!

What do you call a fish without an eye?
A fsh!

What sleeps at the bottom of the sea?
A kipper!

How do you make a goldfish old?
Take away the "g"!

"Now what on **earth** would that be?" asked the Pelican. "I have heard of a **fish-pie** and a **fish-cake** and a **fish-finger**, but I have never heard of a **fish-monger**. Are these **mongers** good to **EAT**?"

What do whales eat? **Fish and ships!**

Where do fish keep their money? **In a riverbank!**

Which part of a fish weighs the most? **The scales!**

Which day do fish hate? **Fryday!**

What do you get from a bad-tempered shark?
You get as far away as possible!

What's the difference between a fish and a piano?
You can't tuna fish!

Which fish only swims at night?
A starfish.

What did the sardine call the submarine?
A can of people.

What do fish take to stay healthy?
Vitamin sea!

Why was the mouse afraid of the water?
Because of the catfish!

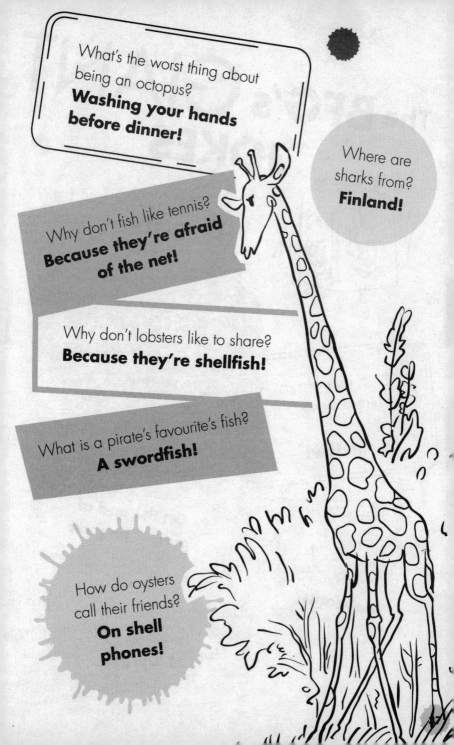

What's the worst thing about being an octopus?
Washing your hands before dinner!

Where are sharks from?
Finland!

Why don't fish like tennis?
Because they're afraid of the net!

Why don't lobsters like to share?
Because they're shellfish!

What is a pirate's favourite's fish?
A swordfish!

How do oysters call their friends?
On shell phones!

The BFG's GIANT JOKES

Giant jokes for **giant** giggles!

How many balls of string would it take to reach the moon?
Just one, if it's long enough!

What is as big as a giant but weighs nothing?
Its shadow!

Where do you find giant snails?
On the end of giants' fingers!

What holds the sun up in the sky?
Sunbeams!

How do you talk to a giant?
Use big words!

Knock knock.
Who's there?
Sarah.
Sarah who?
Sarah giant living here?

What do you call a fear of giants?
Fee-fi-phobia!

Why is there always a conversation going on in the garden?
Because Jack and the beans talk.

How do you greet a three-headed giant?
Politely!

What is higher than a giant?
His hat!

The **Giant** let out a bellow of LAUGHTER. "Just because I is a **giant**, you think I is a MAN-GOBBLING cannybull!" he shouted.

What do you call a giant's raincoat? **A tent!**

What do you call a giant's shoes? **Boats!**

What did the giant say to the lion? **"Here, kitty kitty!"**

What is even higher than a giant? **A giant's hat!**

What bugs bother giants?
Gi-ants!

What do giants call little girls?
Dinner!

What do giants call little boys?
Dessert!

What's a giant's favourite type of bean?
A human bean!

Who is the BFG's biggest enemy?
It's hard to say – they're all giant!

FUNNY **BUGS**

Laughs with **bite!**

What did the slug say as he slipped down the window very fast?
"How slime flies!"

What reads and lives underground?
A bookworm!

What do you do when two snails have a fight?
Leave them to slug it out!

What is the strongest animal in the world?
A snail, because it carries its house on its back!

What did the dog say to the flea?
"Stop bugging me!"

What did the snail say when he got on the turtle's shell?
"Wheeeeeeeeeeeeeeeeeeeeeeeeeeeee!"

How do fleas get around?
They itch-hike!

Why was the Centipede late for the football match?
It took ages to put on its football boots!

What do you call two spiders who just got married?
Newlywebs!

What bugs sing a lot?
Humbugs!

What do you call little bugs who live on the moon?
Lunar-ticks!

What do you call a fly without wings?
A walk!

Where would you put an injured insect?
Into an ant-bulance!

"Stop PULLING the Earthworm's leg," the Ladybug said. This sent the Centipede into hysterics. "Pulling his leg!" he cried, wriggling with glee and pointing at the Earthworm. "Which leg am I PULLING? You tell me that!"

What's the brightest insect?
A firefly!

Why did the fly fly?
Because the spider spied 'er!

What kind of bug does a cowboy ride?
A horsefly!

What do you do
with a bee who's
hurt his wing?
**Take him to a
wasp-ital!**

What are caterpillars
scared of?
Dog-erpillars!

Who won the fight between two silkworms?
It was a tie!

What's the difference between an
elephant and a flea?
**An elephant can have
fleas, but a flea can't have
elephants!**

Why couldn't the butterfly go to the dance?
Because it was a moth-ball!

What do you call a snail on a ship?
A snailor!

How does a firefly race start?
Ready, set, glow!

What did one frog say to the other?
"Time's fun when you're having flies!"

Who is a bee's favourite composer?
Bee-thoven!

The ENORMOUS CROCO-SMILE!

Get your **teeth** into these!

What would the Enormous Crocodile be called if he was a detective?
An investi-gator!

What do you call a thieving alligator?
A crook-odile!

What has four legs, a trunk and sunglasses?
The Enormous Crocodile on holiday!

Why don't crocodiles like fast food?
Because they can't catch it!

What's worse than a crocodile coming to dinner?
Two crocodiles coming to dinner!

The Enormous Crocodile laughed SO much his teeth RATTLED together like pennies in a piggy bank. "Crocodiles don't eat BERRIES," he said. "We eat little boys and girls."

What do crocodiles call children? **Appetizers!**

What's worse than two crocodiles coming to dinner? **Three crocodiles coming to dinner!**

What do you call a crocodile who likes to go bowling? **An alley-gator!**

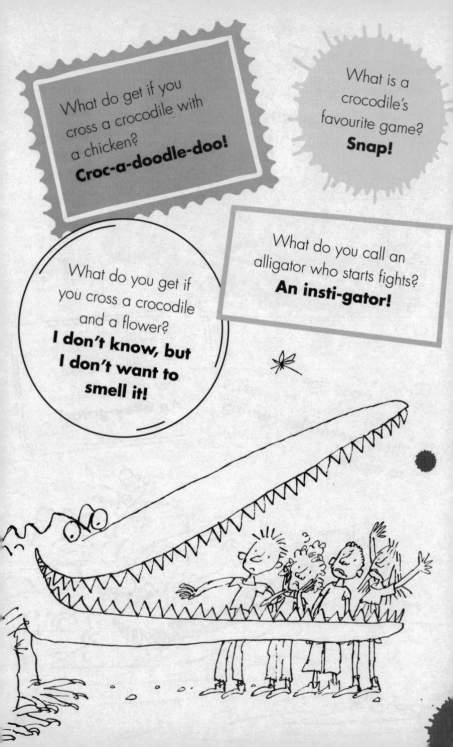

Is it true that a crocodile won't attack you if you're carrying a torch? **It depends how fast you're carrying it!**

Why did the alligator get angry with his friend for crying? **They were just crocodile tears!**

CUSTOMER: I'd like to order some crocodile boots please.
ASSISTANT: **No problem. What size boots does your crocodile wear?**

If a crocodile makes shoes, what do bananas make? **Slippers!**

Trunky's
JUMBO JOKES

For **kids** of any age – it's **irr-elephant!**

How are elephants and trees alike?
They both have trunks!

What do you call an elephant in a phone booth?
Stuck!

What did the peanut say to the elephant?
Nothing, peanuts don't talk!

What time is it when an elephant sits on your bed?
Time to get a new bed!

Where does an elephant pack his luggage?
In his trunk!

Why did the elephant leave the circus?
He was tired of working for peanuts.

What time is it when ten elephants are chasing another elephant?
Ten to one!

Then, with a **crashing** of branches, Trunky the Elephant came **rushing** out of the **jungle**. "That's **not** a bench you were going to **sit** on!" he bellowed. "It's the **Enormous Crocodile**, and he **wants** to **EAT** you **all** up!"

Why are elephants wrinkly?
Because they don't fit on an ironing board!

What game do elephants play when riding in the back of a car?
Squash!

What is the biggest sort of ant?
An eleph-ant!

What do you get when you cross an elephant and a fish?
Swimming trunks!

How do you know when an elephant has been in your refrigerator?
There are footprints in the butter!

What do you do with a green elephant?
Wait until it ripens!

What is big and grey and protects you from the rain?
An umbr-elephant!

What should you give an elephant who's going to be sick?
Plenty of space!

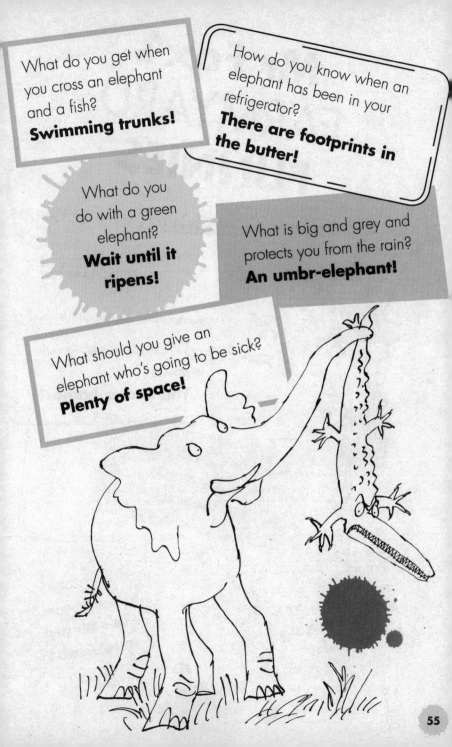

Mr Fox's
FARMYARD
FUNNIES

Shhh! Don't let Boggis, Bunce and Bean hear you **giggling!**

Where do sheep go on holiday?
The Baaaa-hamas!

What do you call a cow that eats your grass?
A lawn moo-er!

What has four legs and goes "Oom, oom"?
A cow walking backwards!

Why do cows go to the theatre?
To see the moo-sicals!

What do you call a pig who knows karate?
A porkchop!

"To Mr Fox!" they all shouted, standing up and raising their GLASSES. "To Mr Fox! Long may he live!"

Why did the lamb cross the road?
To get to the baaaa-rber shop!

What do you call a pig that's been arrested for dangerous driving?
A road hog!

What do you call a cow in a tornado?
A milkshake!

What do you call a sleeping bull?
A bulldozer!

What do you call a cow that twitches?
Beef jerky!

What is the difference between a car and a bull?
A car only has one horn!

What did one cow say to the other?
"Mooooooove over!"

What was the first animal in space?
The cow that jumped over the moon!

What is the easiest way to count a herd of cattle?
With a cow-culator!

What did the farmer call the cow that wouldn't give him any milk?
An udder failure!

Why did the policeman give the sheep a parking ticket?
He was a baaaad driver.

Why did the policeman give the sheep another ticket?
He made an illegal ewe turn!

What is a cow's favourite place?
The mooseum!

What has four wheels, gives milk and eats grass.
A cow on a skateboard!

What does a calf become after it's one year old?
Two years old.

COW: Moooove over!
SHEEP: **Naaaa!**

What do you give a pig with a rash?
Oinkment!

Where do cows go on Saturday night?
To the moooovies!

Why did the pig go "moo"?
Because it was learning a second language!

What do you get when you cross a dinosaur and a pig?
Jurassic pork!

What do you get from a pampered cow?
Spoiled milk!

How many sheep do you need to make a sweater?
None – sheep can't knit!

Where do horses live?
In the neigh-bourhood!

What do you call a pig with no legs?
A groundhog!

What is a horse's favourite sport?
Stable tennis!

Muggle-Wump's
MONKEY
BUSINESS

Monkey around telling your friends these **jokes!**

What do you call an exploding monkey?
A baboom!

What did the banana do when the monkey chased it?
The banana split!

What did the angry monkey do?
He went bananas!

What do you call a massive gorilla?
Sir!

How do monkeys get down the stairs?
They slide down the banana-ster!

What is an ape's favourite cookie?
Chocolate chimp!

Why did the monkey like the banana?
Because it had appeal!

Where should a monkey go when she loses her tail?
To a re-tailer!

How do you catch a monkey?
Climb a tree and act like a banana!

What kind of key opens a banana?
A monkey!

How do you make a gorilla stew? **Keep it waiting for two hours!**

Where do chimps get their gossip from? **The ape-vine!**

"Ah-ha!" cried Muggle-Wump. "Now for the fun! Now for the greatest UPSIDE-DOWN trick of all time! Are you ready?"

What do you call a flying monkey? **A hot-air baboon!**

What do you call a monkey selling potato chips?
A chip-munk!

What do monkeys do for a laugh?
Tell each other jokes about children!

Where do baby monkeys sleep?
In their ape-ricots!

What do you call a baby ape?
A chimp off the old block!

What do apes use to fix their houses?
Monkey wrenches!

Why shouldn't you get into a fight with an ape?
They use gorilla warfare!

When do monkeys fall from the sky?
During Ape-ril showers!

What do chimps wear when they're cooking?
Ape-rons!

Why do apes tell such bad stories?
Because they have no tails!

Why are apes so noisy?
They were raised in a zoo!

Why did the monkey put a net over his head?
He wanted to catch his breath!

Why did the giant ape climb up the skyscraper?
The lift was broken!

Why do gorillas have big nostrils?
Because they have big fingers!

What do you call a gorilla in a tree?
Branch manager!

Dirty Beasts and ANIMAL ANTICS

Funnier than a **trip** to the **zoo!**

What did the snake say when he was offered a piece of cheese?
"Thank you, I'll just have a slither."

Why do animals wear fur coats?
Because they would look silly in plastic macs!

What do you do if your dog chews up a dictionary?
Take the words out of his mouth!

What do you call a girl with a frog on her head?
Lily!

What goes tick-tock, bow-wow, tick-tock, bow-wow?
A watch dog!

Where do mice moor their boats?
At the hickory dickory dock.

What is a cat's favourite movie?
The Sound of Mew-sic!

How does a dog stop a video?
He presses the paws button!

What is it called when you lend money to a bison?
A buff-a-loan!

On which side do tigers have the most stripes?
The outside!

"She is the **Giraffe!**" the Pelican answered. "Is she not **wonderful**? Her **LEGS** are on the **ground** floor and her **head** is looking **out** of the **top WINDOW!**"

What is a cheetah's favourite meal? **Fast food!**

What happened to the frog's car? **It got toad away!**

Why was the cat afraid of the tree? **Because of the bark!**

What does a cat say when somebody steps on its tail? **"Me-ow!"**

What do you get when you plant a frog?
A cr-oak tree!

How do you stop a dog barking on the back seat of a car?
Put him on the front seat!

What is the quietest kind of a dog?
A hush puppy!

How is a dog like a telephone?
It has collar ID!

Why do cows wear bells?
Because their horns don't work!

What did the carrot say to the rabbit?
"Do you want to grab a bite?"

What kind of cat should you never play games with?
A cheetah!

What is black and white and red all over?
A panda with a rash!

Why are giraffes so slow to apologize?
It takes them a long time to swallow their pride!

What do you call a dog that likes bubble baths?
A sham-poodle!

How did Noah see the animals in the ark at night?
With flood lights!

What happened when the lion ate the comedian?
He felt funny!

What's black and white and red all over?
A blushing zebra!

What did the mother buffalo say to her son before he went to school?
"Bison!"

What do you get when you cross a ball of wool and a kangaroo?
A woolly jumper!

What kind of dog always runs a fever?
A hot dog!

What do you do if your cat swallows your pencil?
Use a pen!

Which pine has the longest needles?
A porcupine!

What kind of cars do cats drive?
Cat-illacs!

What do you call a deer with no eyes?
No eye-deer!

There were ten cats in a boat and one jumped out. How many were left?
None – they were all copycats!

What's black and white and red all over?
A sunburnt zebra!

What is a young dog's favourite kind of pizza?
Pupperoni!

How does a mouse feel after it takes a shower?
Squeaky clean!

What do camels use to hide themselves?
Camel-flage!

What do you get if you cross an owl with a lion?
A growl!

What do you call a messy hippo?
A hippopota-mess!

What is
a frog's favourite
year?
A leap year!

What do you call a
pile of kittens?
A meow-ntain!

What does a frog say
when it washes a window?
"Rub it, rub it, rub it!"

Why did the
pony go to the
doctor?
**He was feeling
a little hoarse!**

Where do felines buy their clothes from?
Cat-alogues!

Where do canines buy their clothes from?
Dog-ologues!

Why are frogs so happy?
Because they eat what bugs them!

What kinds of books do rabbits like to read?
Books with hoppy endings!

When a duck has no money, what does he say to the waiter?
"Just put it on my bill!"

Where do penguins go to dance?
The snow ball!

Squirrel NUTS

Nuttier than **Wonka's** Nutty Crunch Surprise!

What do you get if you cross a suitcase and a squirrel?
A nut-case!

Where did the squirrel store his food?
In his pan-tree!

How do you catch a squirrel?
Climb up a tree and act like a nut!

How do you catch a sophisticated squirrel?
Climb up a tree and act like a cashew nut!

What do squirrels eat on holiday?
Coconuts!

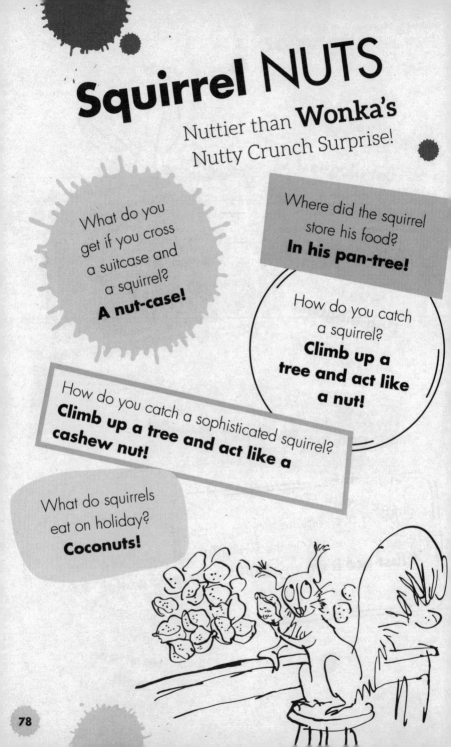

Why did the red squirrel ask for help with some work? **It was a bit of a grey area!**

"All right," said Mr Wonka, "stop here for a moment and catch your BREATH, and take a peek through the glass panel of this door. But don't go in! Whatever you do, don't go into THE NUT ROOM! If you go in, you'll disturb the SQUIRRELS!"

Why couldn't the squirrel eat the walnut? **It was one tough nut to crack!**

Why do woodland animals not eat all their food in one go? **They like to squirrel it away!**

Why did the squirrel take apart the car? **To get down to the nuts and bolts!**

Why can't you be friends with a squirrel? **They drive everyone nuts!**

JOKES for TWITS!

WARNING: These jokes **pong!**

How do you keep a skunk from smelling?
Hold its nose!

How many skunks does it take to make a big stink?
A phew!

Why does a giraffe have such a long neck?
Because its feet stink!

Why do skunks like old movies? **Because they are black and white.**

What I am **trying** to tell **you is that Mr Twit** was a **foul** and **SMELLY** old man.

My dog has no nose. How does he smell? **Awful!**

Why can't you hear a pterodactyl going to the toilet? **Because it has a silent 'p'!**

What did one eye say to the other? **"Between you and me, something smells."**

What's black and white, black and white, black and white and green? **Three skunks fighting over a pickle!**

What did one
snowman say to
the other?
**"Do you smell
carrots?"**

What sorts of books do
skunks like to read?
Best-smellers!

Why is your nose in the middle of your face?
Because it's the scent-er.

What always smells best at the
dinner table?
Your nose!

What did one toilet
say to the other?
**"You look
flushed!"**

What colour socks do bears wear?
They don't wear socks – they go around with bear feet!

Did you hear the joke about the gym sock?
You wouldn't want to – it absolutely stinks!

If athletes get athlete's foot, what do fighter pilots get?
Missile-toe!

What does a pirate call the pattern on his smelly socks?
Arrrrrrrr-gyle!

Why did the pig take a bath?
The farmer said "hogwash"!

Why shouldn't you tease eggs about their smell? **They can't take a yolk!**

What do you call a helicopter with a skunk for a pilot? **A smelly-copter!**

What has a bottom at the top? **Your legs!**

What's the difference between cabbage and bogies? **Kids don't eat cabbage!**

What did the dog say after his third bath? **"Why do I still smell like a wet dog?"**

What do you get if you cross a skunk with a boomerang?
A bad smell that keeps coming back!

Why did the man hate hearing jokes about his feet?
They were too corny!

What do you call a dinosaur with smelly feet?
Ex-stinked!

What did the smelly judge say?
"Odour in court!"

The MOST MONSTROUS Gags EVER!

By **gumfrog!**
These ones are frighteningly **funny.**

How can you tell the difference between a rabbit and a red-eyed monster?
Just try getting a red-eyed monster into a rabbit hutch.

What do you do with a green monster?
Put it in the sun until it ripens!

Why did the monster paint himself in rainbow colours?
Because he wanted to hide in the crayon box

What do you give a monster with big feet? **Big slippers!**

"**Look** out!" cried the **BFG**. "It's the **BLOODBOTTLER!**"

Why was the big, hairy, two-headed monster top of the class at school? **Because two heads are better than one!**

What did the big, hairy monster do when he lost a hand? **He went to the second-hand shop!**

How do you stop a monster digging up your garden? **Take his spade away!**

What does a polite monster say when he meets you for the first time?
"Pleased to eat you!"

Why did all the food get eaten at the monster's party?
Because everyone was goblin!

What kind of monster can sit on the end of your finger?
The bogeyman!

Why did the big, hairy monster give up boxing?
Because he didn't want to spoil his looks!

What happens if a big, hairy monster sits in front of you at the cinema? **You miss most of the film!**

Why did the two cyclopses fight? **They could never see eye to eye on anything!**

How do you know when there's a monster under your bed? **Your nose touches the ceiling!**

What is the best way to speak to a monster? **From a long distance!**

Why did the monster have green ears and a red nose? **So that he could hide in rhubarb patches!**

How do you tell a good monster from a bad one? **If it's a good one you will be able to talk about it later!**

What's big, heavy, furry, dangerous and has sixteen wheels? **A monster on roller-skates!**

What do you call a huge, ugly, slobbering, furry monster with cotton wool in his ears? **Anything you like – he can't hear you!**

Why couldn't the swamp monster go to the party? **Because he was bogged down in his work!**

Who won the witch beauty contest? **No one!**

How do you know that there's a monster in your bath? **You can't get the shower curtain closed!**

How do you get six monsters in a biscuit tin? **Take the biscuits out first!**

Why was the monster standing on his head? **He was turning things over in his mind!**

What should you do if a monster runs through your front door? **Run through the back door!**

What do little vampires learn at school?
The alpha-bat!

What sort of monster loves to party?
The boogie-man!

Why are monsters so forgetful?
Everything goes in one ear and out the five others!

What did the monster say about his eight arms?
They come in very handy!

What do monsters like in their sandwiches?
Ghoul-slaw!

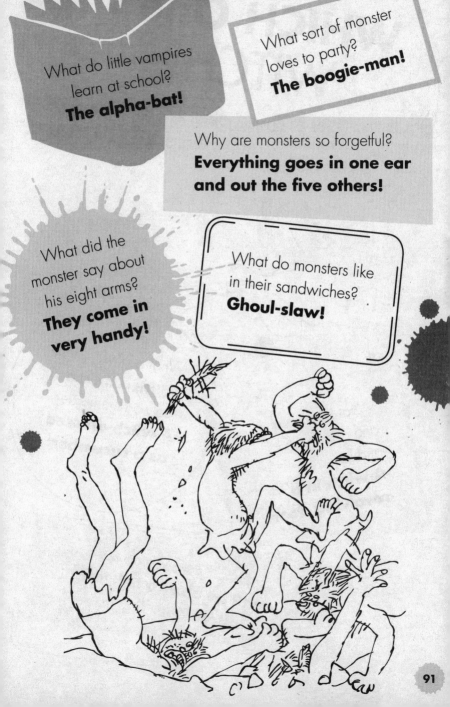

WHICH One's WITCH?

These jokes are the Grand High Witch's worst **nightmare!**

How did the witch look after she was run over by a car?
Tyred!

What is green on the outside and evil and ugly on the inside?
A witch dressed as a cucumber!

What is evil, ugly and goes round and round?
A witch in a revolving door!

What happens if you see twin witches?
You won't be able to tell which witch is witch!

What does a witch get if she is a poor traveller?
Broom sick!

Why did the witch put her broom in the wash?
She wanted a clean sweep!

Why did the stupid witch keep her clothes in the fridge?
She liked to have something cool to slip into in the evenings!

Why did the witch give up fortune telling?
There was no future in it!

What has six legs and flies?
A witch giving her cat a ride!

What has handles and flies?
A witch in a dustbin!

What is evil, ugly and bounces?
A witch on a trampoline!

What did the doctor say to the witch in hospital?
With any luck you'll soon be well enough to get up for a spell!

How do witches lose weight?
They join Weight Witches!

What do witches race on?
Vroom-sticks!

Have you heard about the good weather witch?
She's forecasting sunny spells!

How is the witch's football team doing?
They're going through a successful spell!

What makes more noise than an angry witch?
Two angry witches!

What happened to the witch with an upside-down nose?
Every time she sneezed, her hat blew off!

What happened when the witch went for a job as a TV presenter? **The producer said that she had the perfect face for radio!**

Why did the witch join the football club? **Because she heard they were looking for a new sweeper!**

What do witches eat for dinner? **Real toad-in-the-hole!**

Who turns the lights off at Halloween? **The lights witch!**

What is the best way of stopping infection from witch bites? **Don't bite any witches!**

What do you call a witch with one leg? **Eileen!**

A real WITCH gets the same pleasure from SQUELCHING a child as you get from eating a plateful of strawberries and thick cream.

What do witches sing at Christmas? **"Deck the halls with poison ivy!"**

What is old, ugly and bright blue? **A witch holding her breath!**

What happens to naughty witches at school? **They get ex-spelled!**

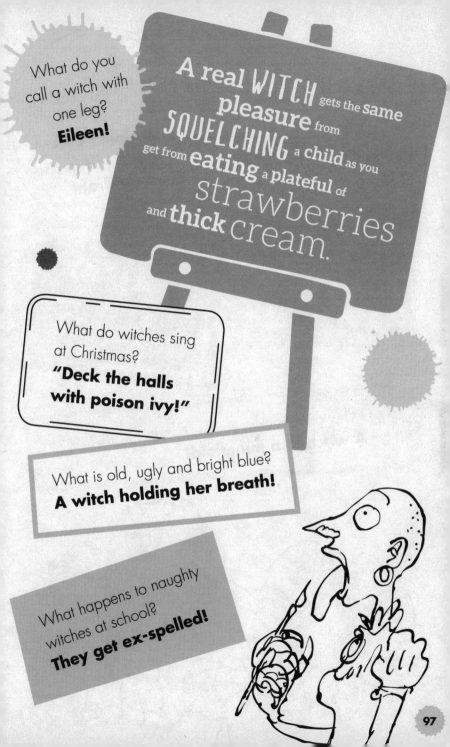

What do you call a witch who likes the beach but is afraid of the water?
A chicken sand-witch!

Why do witches like cooking with toads' legs?
A child's legs wouldn't fit in the cauldron!

What do you get if you cross a witch and an iceberg?
A cold spell!

What do you call a nice, friendly witch?
A failure!

What goes cackle, cackle, cackle . . . BOOM?
A witch in a minefield!

What is a witch with hay fever called?
An itchy witchy!

What's the best way of talking to a witch?
Over the phone!

Why didn't the witch sing at the concert?
She had a frog in her throat!

What do you call it when a witch's cat falls off her broomstick?
A cat-astrophe!

What has six legs and flies?
Three witches on one broomstick!

Formula 86
FUNNIES

Make your friends **squeak** with **laughter!**

What do cats call mice on skateboards?
Meals on wheels!

What do angry mice send each other at Christmas?
Cross-mouse cards!

When is it unlucky to see a black cat cross your path?
When you're a mouse!

What did the cat have for breakfast?
Mice crispies!

What goes dot-dot-dash-squeak?
Mouse code!

What is a mouse's favourite game?
Hide and squeak!

Who are small, furry and good with swords?
The Three Mouse-keteers!

How do you save a drowning mouse?
Mouse-to-mouse resuscitation!

When is it time to oil your mouse?
When it starts squeaking!

What do you get when you lock mice in the freezer?
Mice cubes!

What do mice like for dessert?
Mice cream!

When do mice need to carry an umbrella?
When it's raining cats and dogs!

Which Roman emperor was actually a mouse?
Julius Cheese-r.

Why is there no such thing as a mousefish?
Because of all the catfish!

What Roman Emperor was also a mouse?
Julius Cheeser!

What do mice do when they're at home?
Mouse-work!

Bruno looked down at his paws. He jumped. "Good grief!" he cried. "I am a MOUSE! You wait till my father hears about this!" "He may think it's an improvement," I said.

What is hairy and lives on a man's face?
A mouse-tache!

How do mice celebrate when they move home?
They throw a mouse-warming party!

Wonka
WISECRACKS

Sweeten up even the most
boring adults!

What do Oompa-Loompas
use to clean their teeth?
Candy floss!

Did you hear the joke about
the chocolate sauce?
**I'm not telling you.
You might spread it!**

What's the best
thing to put into a
chocolate bar?
Your teeth!

What is better than seeing
a chocolate river?
**Drinking a chocolate
river!**

What did the bubblegum say to the shoe? **"I'm stuck on you!"**

Why was the biscuit sad? **She was feeling crumby!**

What do Oompa-Loompas make sandwiches with? **Shortbread!**

What kind of bear has no teeth? **A gummy bear!**

"My **dear boy**," said Grandpa Joe, raising himself up a little HIGHER on his pillow, "Mr Willy Wonka is the most amazing, the most **fantastic**, the most extraordinary chocolate maker the world has **ever** seen! I thought **everybody** knew that!"

What do you call a lamb covered in chocolate?
A chocolate baaaa!

What sort of keys do kids like to carry around with them?
Coo-keys!

Why did the cake lorry get stuck?
Because of the rocky road!

Why did the custard cream go to the dentist? **Because it lost its filling!**

What happened to the chocolate factory? **It melted!**

What kind of sweet is never on time? **Choco-late!**

Where do you go to learn how to make ice cream? **Sundae school!**

How do you make milk shake? **Give it a fright!**

Knock knock!
Who's there?
Banana!
Banana who?
Banana split so ice creamed!

Why is baking cruel?
Because you beat the eggs and whip the cream!

What did the doughnut wear to bed?
Jammies!

How do you make an apple turnover?
Push it down a hill!

What cake is so hard it breaks your teeth?
Marble cake!

Why do you put candles on the top of a birthday cake?
It would be too difficult to put them on the bottom!

What did the newspaper say to the ice cream?
"What's the scoop?"

What do you give a sick lemon?
Lemon-aid!

How do astronauts eat their ice cream?
In floats!

Why did the giant put clouds in his pancakes?
To make them light and fluffy!

MORE JOKES for TWITS!

WARNING: These jokes get **hairy!**

What do you call a goat with a beard?
Goatee!

What did the man say to his barber?
"I moustache you a question, but I'll shave it for later."

Who shaves ten times a day and still has a beard?
The barber!

What happens when bearded men sunbathe?
They get sideburns!

Mr Twit felt that his hairiness made him look terrifically **wise** and grand. But in truth he was neither of these things. **Mr Twit** was a twit. He was born a twit. And **now** at the age of sixty, he was a **BIGGER** twit than ever.

What did the man say about his enormous beard?
"It just grew on me!"

How do barbers make phone calls?
They cut them short!

Why did Mr Twit put a rabbit on his head?
He wanted a full head of hare!

Why are people always asking Mr Twit to turn round?
They can't tell which side of him is which!

What do you call a pen with no hair?
A bald point!

Who never gets their hair wet in the shower?
A bald man!

Why did the bald man go outside?
To get some fresh hair!

Why doesn't Mr Twit want to shave his beard?
He's rather attached to it!

What kind of beard does the sea have?
Wavy!

What's the difference between Mr Twit's beard and a fridge?
The food in a fridge is fresh!

Why do barbers make good drivers?
Because they know all the short cuts!

Matilda MAGIC!

Funnies to make your friends cry ... with **laughter!**

Did you hear about the magic tractor?
It turned into a field!

In what way is Miss Trunchbull mean but fair?
She's mean to EVERYONE!

What do you call a fortune-teller who has escaped from prison?
A medium at large!

Why did Miss Trunchbull give her whole class a zero on their tests?
She couldn't give them anything lower!

"Do YOU think that all children's books ought to have FUNNY bits in them?" Miss Honey asked.

"I do," Matilda said. "Children are NOT so serious as grown-ups and they LOVE to LAUGH."

Why is your newt called Tiny?
Because he's my-newt!

Why did the clock get sent to see the Trunchbull?
For tocking too much!

TRUNCHBULL: Why aren't you standing at the end of the line like I told you?

PUPIL: **I tried, but there was somebody standing there already!**

What's the difference between a hungry man and Bruce Bogtrotter? **One longs to eat and the other eats too long!**

What did the bookworm say to the librarian? **"Please may I burrow this book?"**

Why was Mr Wormwood angry when Matilda put glue in his hat? **It was a hat trick!**

MISS HONEY: You missed school yesterday, didn't you? LAVENDER: **No, I didn't miss it in the slightest!**

What is Miss Honey's favourite nation? **Expla-nation!**

Why was the maths book always unhappy? **Because it had lots of problems!**

DAD: What did you learn at school today? SON: **Not enough – they said I have to go back again tomorrow!**

Why did the music teacher need a ladder? **To reach the high notes!**

What kind of schoolbag is always tired? **A knapsack!**

Why did Bruce Bogtrotter eat his homework? **The teacher told him it was a piece of cake!**

And finally . . .

THE **Whizzpoppers!**

According to the BFG,
whizzpopping is a sign of
happiness!

What's the difference between
a symphony and a whizzpop?
**One is music to your ear
and the other is music
from your rear!**

What do you get if you
cross onions and beans?
Tear gas!

What did the poker
player say when he let
out a whizzpop?
**"I've played my
trump card!"**

What's
invisible and smells
like carrots?
**A bunny
whizzpop!**

Why is a whizzpop the sharpest thing in the world?
It can go through almost any fabric and it never leaves a hole!

"**Kings** and Queens are **WHIZZPOPPING**. Presidents are **WHIZZPOPPING**. Glamorous film stars are **WHIZZPOPPING**. Little **babies** are **WHIZZPOPPING**. But where **I** come from, it is **not** polite to talk about it."

What are the queen's whizzpops made of?
Noble gas!

Somewhere in the world a person whizzpops every other second.
We must find this person and stop them!

Did you hear about the man who was giving out anti-whizzpop leaflets?
He accidentally let one rip!

Why couldn't the skeleton whizzpop?
It didn't have the guts to do it!

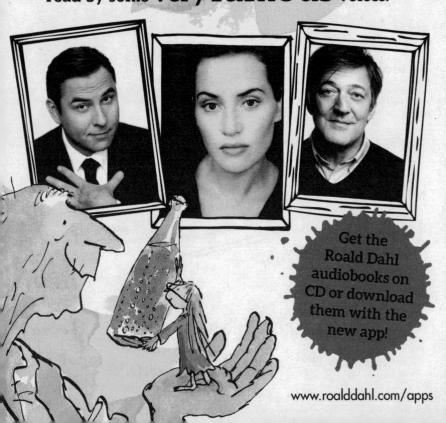

Have **YOU** PLAYED the **FANTASTICALLY** FUN **NEW** **ROALD DAHL** apps?

www.roalddahl.com/apps

ROALD DAHL DAY

CELEBRATE

THE PHIZZ-WHIZZING WORLD of ROALD DAHL

EVERY YEAR on

13th SEPTEMBER!

JOIN THE PARTY AT
www.roalddahl.com

STORIES ARE GOOD FOR YOU.

Roald Dahl said,
*'If you have good thoughts, they will shine
out of your face like sunbeams and you
will always look lovely.'*

We believe in doing good things.
That's why ten per cent of all Roald Dahl income*
goes to our charity partners. We have supported causes
including: specialist children's nurses, grants for
families in need, and educational outreach programmes.
Thank you for helping us to sustain this vital work.

Find out more at roalddahl.com

The only thing more
fun than a good joke,
is a good whizzpop!

FROBSCOTTLE
and
WHIZZPOPPERS

'Burping is filthsome,' the BFG said. 'Us giants is never doing it.'

'But with *your* drink,' Sophie said, 'what was it you called it?'

'Frobscottle,' said the BFG.

'With frobscottle,' Sophie said, 'the bubbles in your tummy will be going *downwards* and that could have a far nastier result.'

'Why nasty?' asked the BFG, frowning.

'Because,' Sophie said, blushing a little, 'if they go down instead of up, they'll be coming out somewhere else with an even louder and ruder noise.'

'A whizzpopper!' cried the BFG, beaming at her. 'Us giants is making whizzpoppers all the time! Whizzpopping is a sign of happiness. It is music in our ears! You surely is not telling me that a little whizzpopping is forbidden among human beans?'

'It is considered extremely rude,' Sophie said.

'But you is whizzpopping, is you not, now and again?' asked the BFG.

'Everyone is whizzpopping, if that's what you call it,' Sophie said. 'Kings and Queens are whizzpopping. Presidents are whizzpopping. Glamorous film stars are whizzpopping. Little babies are whizzpopping. But where I come from, it is not polite to talk about it.'

'Redunculous!' said the BFG. 'If everyone is making

whizzpoppers, then why not talk about it? We is now having a swiggle of this delicious frobscottle and you will see the happy result.' The BFG shook the bottle vigorously. The pale green stuff fizzed and bubbled. He removed the cork and took a tremendous gurgling swig.

'It's glummy!' he cried. 'I love it!'

For a few moments, the Big Friendly Giant stood quite still, and a look of absolute ecstasy began to spread over his long wrinkly face. Then suddenly the heavens opened and he let fly with a series of the loudest and rudest noises Sophie had ever heard in her life. They reverberated around the walls of the cave like thunder and the glass jars rattled on their shelves. But most astonishing of all, the force of the explosions actually lifted the enormous giant clear off his feet, like a rocket.

'*Whoopee!*' he cried, when he came down to earth again. 'Now *that* is whizzpopping for you!'

Sophie burst out laughing. She couldn't help it.

'Have some yourself!' cried the BFG, tipping the neck of the enormous bottle towards her.

'Don't you have a cup?' Sophie said.

'No cups. Only bottle.'

Sophie opened her mouth, and very gently the BFG tipped the bottle forward and poured some of the fabulous frobscottle down her throat.

And oh gosh, how delicious it was! It was sweet and refreshing. It tasted of vanilla and cream, with just the faintest trace of raspberries on the edge of the flavour. And the bubbles were wonderful. Sophie could actually feel them bouncing and bursting all around her tummy. It was an amazing sensation. It felt as though hundreds of tiny people were dancing a jig inside her and tickling her with their toes. It was lovely.

'It's lovely!' she cried.

'Just wait,' said the BFG, flapping his ears.

Sophie could feel the bubbles travelling lower and lower down her tummy, and then suddenly, inevitably . . . the explosion came. The trumpets sounded and she too made the walls of the cavern ring with the sound of music and thunder.

'Bravo!' shouted the BFG, waving the bottle. 'You is very good for a beginner! Let's have some more!'

That's it.
The end of the book.

HERE IS
one LAST **WORD**,
invented by **Roald Dahl** HIMSELF.
Make sure you KEEP IT SAFE.

BUGGLES

Adjective: Used to describe someone who's

completely crazy!

ROALD
DAHL